I am
Rosa Parks

BRAD MELTZER

illustrated by Christopher Eliopoulos

DIAL BOOKS FOR YOUNG READERS an imprint of Penguin Group (USA) LLC

I am **Rosa Parks.**

Growing up, I was small for my age.
I was sick a lot too, since we didn't have money for a doctor.
But that didn't mean I was weak.

When I was eleven, as I was walking home from school, a boy on roller skates came zipping by and shoved me. He thought I'd be an easy target.

To his surprise, I turned around and pushed him back.

I knew fighting was wrong. But I didn't want him picking on me again.

UH-OH. THIS IS GONNA BE BAD.

DID YOU JUST PUSH MY SON?

His mother saw what happened. She was mad that I'd pushed him.

I stood my ground.
And calmly, but firmly, I explained . . .

I wasn't just standing up to that mom. Or even to the
boy on roller skates.
I was standing up for myself.
After that, the boy and his mom never bothered me again.
Still, it's hard to change things. Sometimes it can take a
long time.

Back then, if you were black, you were treated unfairly just because of the color of your skin.

You weren't allowed to live in the same neighborhood as a white person, eat in the same restaurant, ride the same elevator, or use the same bathroom.

You couldn't even drink from the same water fountain. One was marked for "Whites"; the other for "Colored."

When I was little, I used to wonder if "white" water tasted different from "colored" water. I even wondered if "colored" water came in lots of colors.

But it didn't.
The only difference was I had to walk outside, or even down the block, to get mine. Of course, it wasn't just about water fountains.

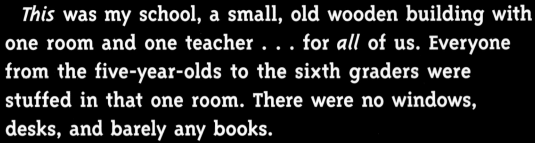

This was my school, a small, old wooden building with one room and one teacher . . . for *all* of us. Everyone from the five-year-olds to the sixth graders were stuffed in that one room. There were no windows, desks, and barely any books.

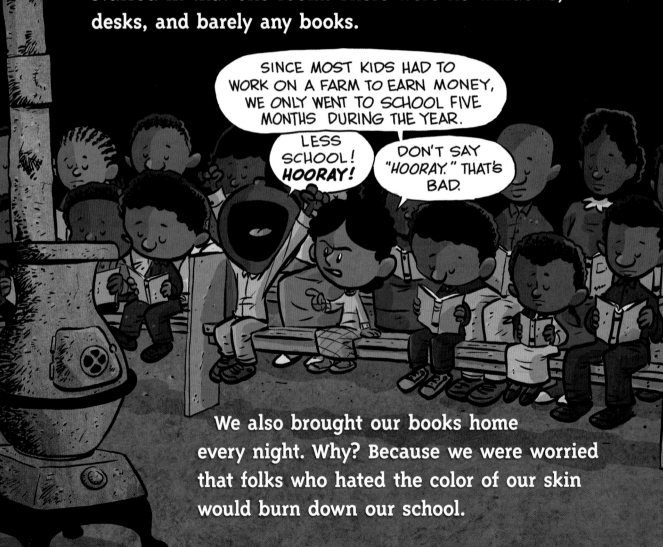

We also brought our books home every night. Why? Because we were worried that folks who hated the color of our skin would burn down our school.

Now, here's the school for the kids who were white.
Notice the difference?
It was a new brick building with beautiful windows, new desks, and plenty of books. Plus a playground.

Also, if you were black, you had to walk to school. If you were white, you got to take a bus.

The worst part was, when I'd walk home with my brother, the kids on the bus would throw trash at us.

It made me feel horrible.

But there were no "civil rights" back then. The only solution was to move off the road.

And really, what kind of solution is that?

As I got older, things didn't change much.

One winter, I was waiting for the local city bus.
If you were black, you had to ride in the back.
If you were white, you rode up front.
On that day, the back of the bus was packed.

The driver didn't care. He wanted me off the bus.
He grabbed me by my coat sleeve.
I dropped my purse near the front door. To pick it up, I sat in the front seat—a white seat. It made the driver madder than ever.

That's what he called it.
"My bus." As if it were his.
The bus *wasn't* his, though.
It belonged to all of us.

From there, in addition to working as a seamstress, I started working to change things.

At the NAACP, we fought for fairer laws, and made sure that people's stories were heard.

I also stopped using "colored" water fountains. I'd rather go thirsty than be treated so poorly.

It was the same with separate elevators. Instead of riding them, I'd take the stairs.

But as for real change . . .

It was the end of a busy Thursday.

I was forty-two years old and on the bus, going home.

This time, I was sitting in the first row of seats that were allowed for black people.

There was one man next to me, and two women across from me.

It was the same driver from before.
The exact same one from all those years earlier.

People say that the reason I refused to give up my seat was because I was tired.

And I was. But it wasn't the kind of tired that came from aching feet.

The only tired I was, was tired of giving in.

I ignited a movement.

From there, the Montgomery Bus Boycott began. For 381 days—that's well over a year—all blacks in the city, and even a few whites, refused to ride the public buses.

Finally, the rules were changed. Public buses were no longer allowed to separate people based on the color of their skin.

That was only the beginning.

Eventually, we were allowed to drink from the same water fountains, ride the same elevators, and yes, go to the same schools.

In the Declaration of Independence, Thomas Jefferson wrote that we're all created equal.

Finally, the nation was starting to act like it.

Of course, that didn't mean the fight was over.
There were thousands of other people just like
that bus driver.

But after hearing how I didn't give up my seat,
there were now thousands more people just like me.
Together. Inspired. And committed to justice.

In my life, people tried to knock me down.
Tried to make me feel less than I was. They teased
me for being small. Being black. Being different.
Let me be clear: No one should be able to do that.

But if they try, you must stand strong.
Stand for what's right.
Stand up for yourself (even if it means sitting down).

When you do . . .

Others will follow.

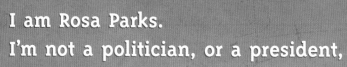

I am Rosa Parks.

I'm not a politician, or a president, or an actor, or a famous business owner.

I'm just an ordinary person.

But I'm also proof that there's *no such thing* as an ordinary person.

I hope you'll always stand up for yourself, and I hope you'll remember that we're all in this together.

"*The only tired I was, was tired of giving in.*"
—ROSA PARKS

 Timeline

FEBRUARY 4, 1913	1943	DECEMBER 1943	DECEMBER 1, 1955
Born in Tuskegee, Alabama	Kicked off a bus for entering through the front door	Became secretary of the Montgomery chapter of the NAACP	Arrested for refusing to give up her seat on the bus

Rosa's police photo, taken in 1956

Rosa after bus segregation was outlawed (1956)

A typical segregated classroom
when Rosa was young

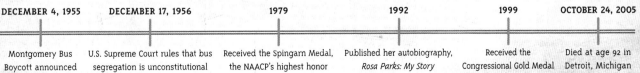

DECEMBER 4, 1955	DECEMBER 17, 1956	1979	1992	1999	OCTOBER 24, 2005
Montgomery Bus Boycott announced	U.S. Supreme Court rules that bus segregation is unconstitutional	Received the Spingarn Medal, the NAACP's highest honor	Published her autobiography, *Rosa Parks: My Story*	Received the Congressional Gold Medal	Died at age 92 in Detroit, Michigan

In memory of
Dotty Rubin,
my Nanny and Grandmother,
who loved her family,
loved her politics,
and always fought for the right side
—B.M.

For my mother, Sandy,
who taught me to treat everyone equally
and gave me my love of history
—C.E.

For historical accuracy, we tried to use Rosa's and the bus driver's actual dialogue. For more of Rosa's true voice, we recommend and acknowledge the autobiography *Rosa Parks: My Story* (see below).

SOURCES
Rosa Parks: My Story by Rosa Parks with Jim Haskins (Dial Books, 1992)
Rosa Parks by Douglas Brinkley (Viking, 2000)
Rosa Parks: Civil Rights Leader by Mary Hull (Chelsea House, 2006)
The Rebellious Life of Mrs. Rosa Parks by Jeanne Theoharis (Beacon Press, 2013)
Don't Know Much About Rosa Parks by Kenneth C. Davis (HarperCollins, 2005)

FURTHER READING FOR KIDS
Rosa by Nikki Giovanni (Henry Holt, 2005)
Back of the Bus by Aaron Reynolds (Philomel, 2010)
I Am Rosa Parks by Rosa Parks (Penguin Young Readers, 1997)
Who Was Rosa Parks? by Yona Zeldis McDonough (Grosset, 2010)

DIAL BOOKS FOR YOUNG READERS
Published by the Penguin Group • Penguin Group (USA) LLC, 375 Hudson Street, New York, New York 10014

USA | Canada | UK | Ireland | Australia | New Zealand | India | South Africa | China
penguin.com

A PENGUIN RANDOM HOUSE COMPANY

Text copyright © 2014 by Forty-four Steps, Inc • Illustrations copyright © 2014 by Christopher Eliopoulos

Library of Congress Cataloging-in-Publication Data. • Meltzer, Brad. I am Rosa Parks / Brad Meltzer ; illustrated by Christopher Eliopoulos. • pages cm. — (Ordinary people change the world). ISBN 978-0-8037-4085-3 (hardcover) • 1. Parks, Rosa, 1913–2005—Juvenile literature. 2. African American women—Alabama—Montgomery—Biography—Juvenile literature. 3. African Americans—Alabama—Montgomery—Biography—Juvenile literature. 4. Civil rights workers—Alabama—Montgomery—Biography—Juvenile literature. 5. African Americans—Civil rights—Alabama—Montgomery—History—20th century—Juvenile literature. 6. Segregation in transportation—Alabama—Montgomery—History—20th century—Juvenile literature. 7. Montgomery (Ala.)—Race relations—Juvenile literature. 8. Montgomery (Ala.)—Biography—Juvenile literature. I. Eliopoulos, Christopher, illustrator. II. Title. • F334.M753P385554 2014 323.092—dc23 [B] 2013034308

Rosa Parks photograph on page 38 courtesy of the Johnson Publishing Company, LLC. Photograph of Rosa sitting on the bus on page 39 courtesy of Corbis. Rosa Parks mug shot on page 39 courtesy of the Associated Press. Segregated classroom photograph on page 39 courtesy of the Library of Congress.

Manufactured in China on acid-free paper • 10 9 8 7 6 5 4 3
Designed by Jason Henry • Text set in Triplex • The artwork for this book was created digitally.

The publisher does not have any control over and does not assume any responsibility for author or third-party websites or their content.

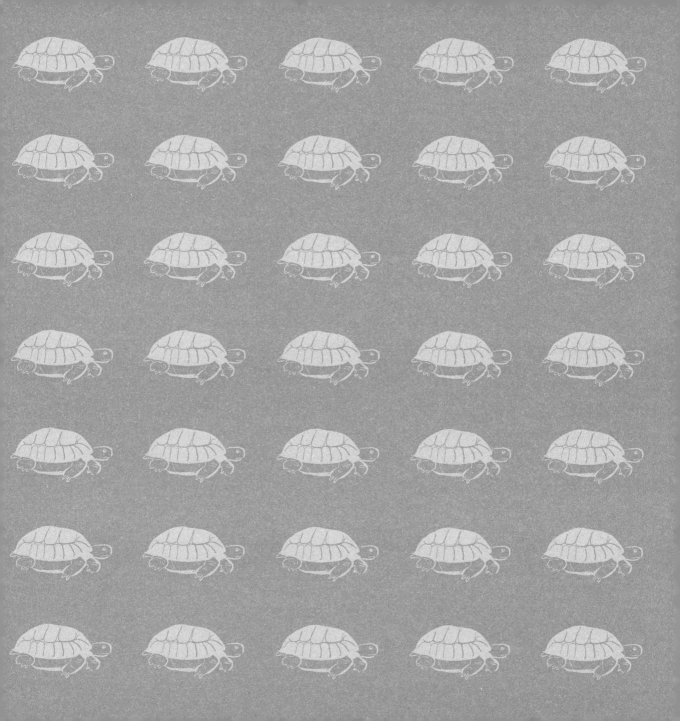

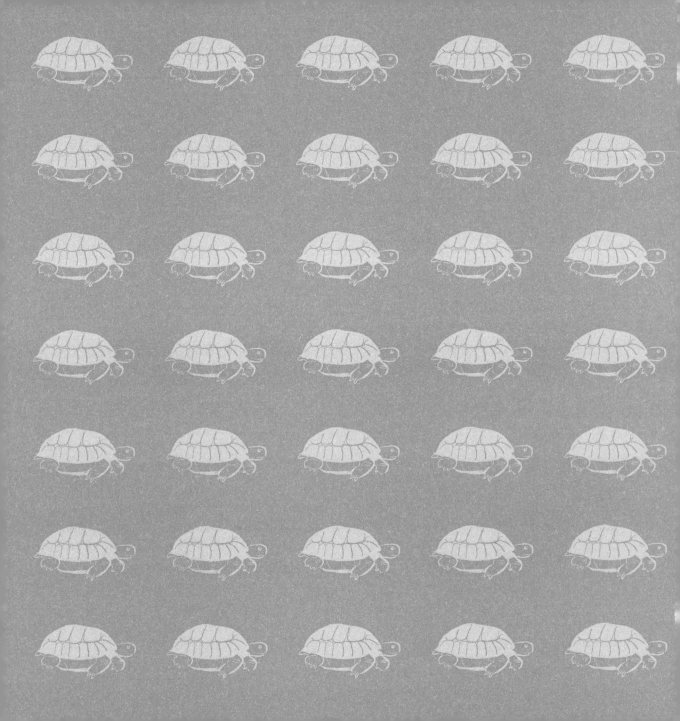

ORDINARY PEOPLE CHANGE the WORLD

I am
Abraham Lincoln

BRAD MELTZER

illustrated by Christopher Eliopoulos

DIAL BOOKS FOR YOUNG READERS an imprint of Penguin Group (USA) LLC

I am **Abraham Lincoln.**

I also loved animals.

When I was ten years old, I saw a group
of boys playing with some turtles.

But as I got closer, I realized they weren't *playing*.
They were taking hot coals and putting them on
top of the turtles, to see what would happen.
To them, it was harmless fun.

In that moment, I could have just walked away.
When you're ten years old, it's hard to do the right thing.
But someone has to.

Those boys let
the turtle go.

Soon after, I wrote one of my first essays—about how hurting animals is wrong.

That may not seem like a big deal, but back then, most kids—and even adults—didn't know how to write.

In fact, the state of Indiana was so new, schools weren't even built yet.

I went to school for barely a year. *Total!*
But that didn't stop me.
Using chalk, I practiced writing the alphabet on trees.
I even wrote in the dirt of the cornfield.

And while waiting
in line at the local
store.

And in one of my
favorite positions:
with my feet up on
a tree.

Before long, I had read every book in the neighborhood, from the Bible to *Aesop's Fables* to *Robinson Crusoe*.
But one of my favorites? A book about George Washington.

Today some may call it a fight, but it was really a wrestling match.

Me against their leader, Jack Armstrong.

Back then the rule was, once you grabbed your opponent, you couldn't break your hold.

But Jack did . . . so he could grab my leg and send me flying.

I wasn't mad I lost. Everyone loses sometimes.
What got me upset?
He had *cheated*!

Within seconds, they all surrounded me.
They were waiting for me to back down. Or to lose my cool.
Instead, calmly and confidently, I told them . . .

They knew I meant it.

Sometimes, the hardest fights don't reveal a winner—
but they do reveal character.
Especially when you're fighting for something you believe in.

Still, not every struggle brought a victory.
Years later, I saw a group of slaves chained
together in a boat on the Ohio River.
Back then, not all people were free.
Some were slaves.

Just because of the color of their skin, they were forced to work without pay. They were treated terribly.

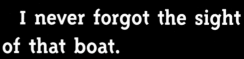

I never forgot the sight of that boat.

I didn't do anything that day, but for years, the memory of those people . . . it haunted me.

I was still thinking about them when I became president.

I lost four elections before I got the big job. Four!

If I had turned my head and looked away,
I would've avoided the fight.
   But if I'd learned anything in life,
it was this:
   When someone needed help,
I wasn't so good at looking away.

The Civil War lasted longer than anyone thought.

The fighting took a terrible toll.

People on our side were ready to give up.

To reenergize them, we held a big event in Gettysburg, Pennsylvania.

Soon after, I helped pass a law that ended slavery in America and freed all those people.
Then we ended the Civil War.

As a result, we didn't just bring together these United States of America—we proved that this government of the people, by the people, and for the people would be dedicated to freedom and justice.

I am Abraham Lincoln.
I will never stop fighting for what's right.
And I hope you'll remember that when you
speak your mind—and speak for others—
there's no more powerful way to be heard.

"I am not bound to win, but I am bound to be true. I am not bound to succeed, but I am bound to live by the light that I have. I must stand with anybody that stands right, and stand with him while he is right, and part with him when he goes wrong."

—ABRAHAM LINCOLN

Timeline

FEBRUARY 12, 1809	1830	1836	NOVEMBER 4, 1842	1847–1849	1858
Born in Hodgenville, Kentucky	Moved to Illinois	Became a lawyer	Married Mary Todd	Served in U.S. House of Representatives	Lost the election for U.S. Senate

During the Civil War, 1862

Replica of Abraham's first home, found at the Lincoln Birthplace National Historical Park in Kentucky

Giving the Gettysburg Address, 1863

NOVEMBER 6, 1860
Elected 16th President of the United States

1861
The Civil War began

JANUARY 1, 1863
Emancipation Proclamation

NOVEMBER 19, 1863
Gettysburg Address

APRIL 14, 1865
Shot by John Wilkes Booth

APRIL 15, 1865
Died in Washington, DC

DECEMBER 6, 1865
Slavery outlawed by Thirteenth Amendment to U.S. Constitution

For Theo & Jonas,
my sons,
may you always fight for what's right,
and for those who need it
–B.M.

For Jeremy & Justin.
Always be strong by helping the weak,
always stand up for those who can't speak,
and even though you're identical,
you will always be unique.
–Dad (C.E.)

Special thanks to Douglas L. Wilson and the Lincoln Studies Center at Knox College in Illinois

SOURCES
Honor's Voice: The Transformation of Abraham Lincoln by Douglas L. Wilson (Knopf, 1998)
Lincoln's Virtues: An Ethical Biography by William Lee Miller (Knopf, 2002)
Lincoln: A Life of Purpose and Power by Richard Carwardine (Knopf, 2006)
Lincoln by David Herbert Donald (Simon & Schuster, 1995)

FURTHER READING FOR KIDS
Abe Lincoln's Hat by Martha Brenner (Random House, 1994)
Who Was Abraham Lincoln? by Janet Pascal (Grosset & Dunlap, 2008)
Just a Few Words, Mr. Lincoln by Jean Fritz (Penguin Young Readers, 1993)
Looking at Lincoln by Maira Kalman (Nancy Paulsen Books, 2012)
Abe Lincoln: The Boy Who Loved Books by Kay Winters (Simon & Schuster, 2003)

DIAL BOOKS FOR YOUNG READERS
Published by the Penguin Group • Penguin Group (USA) LLC, 375 Hudson Street, New York, New York 10014

USA | Canada | UK | Ireland | Australia | New Zealand | India | South Africa | China
penguin.com

A PENGUIN RANDOM HOUSE COMPANY

Text copyright © 2014 by Forty-four Steps, Inc. • Illustrations copyright © 2014 by Christopher Eliopoulos

Library of Congress Cataloging-in-Publication Data
Meltzer, Brad. • I am Abraham Lincoln/Brad Meltzer; illustrated by Christopher Eliopoulos. • pages cm. — (Ordinary people change the world) • ISBN 978-0-8037-4083-9 (hardcover: acid-free paper) • 1. Lincoln, Abraham, 1809–1865—Juvenile literature. 2. Presidents—United States—Biography—Juvenile literature. 3. United States—History—Civil War, 1861–1865—Juvenile literature. 4. United States—Politics and government—1861–1865—Juvenile literature. I. Eliopoulos, Christopher, illustrator. II. Title. • E457.905.M45 2014 973.7092—dc23 [B] 2013016424

Photograph of Abraham Lincoln on page 38, image of Lincoln giving the Gettysburg Address on page 39, and photo in front of a tent (on the battlefield of Antietam) on page 39 courtesy of the Library of Congress • Cabin photo on page 39 from the Abraham Lincoln Birthplace National Historical Park in Hodgenville, Kentucky, courtesy of the Library of Congress

Manufactured in China on acid-free paper • 10 9 8 7 6 5
Designed by Jason Henry • Text set in Triplex • The artwork for this book was created digitally.

The publisher does not have any control over and does not assume any responsibility for author or third-party websites or their content.

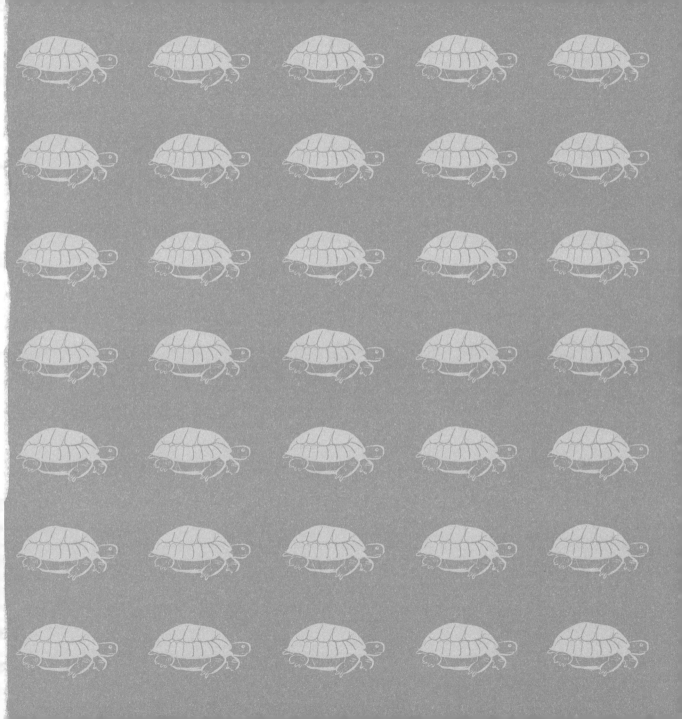

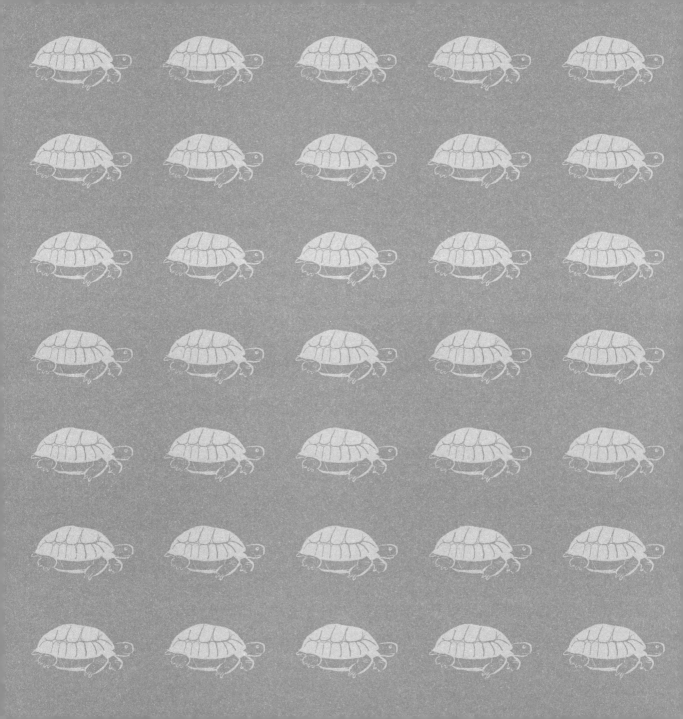

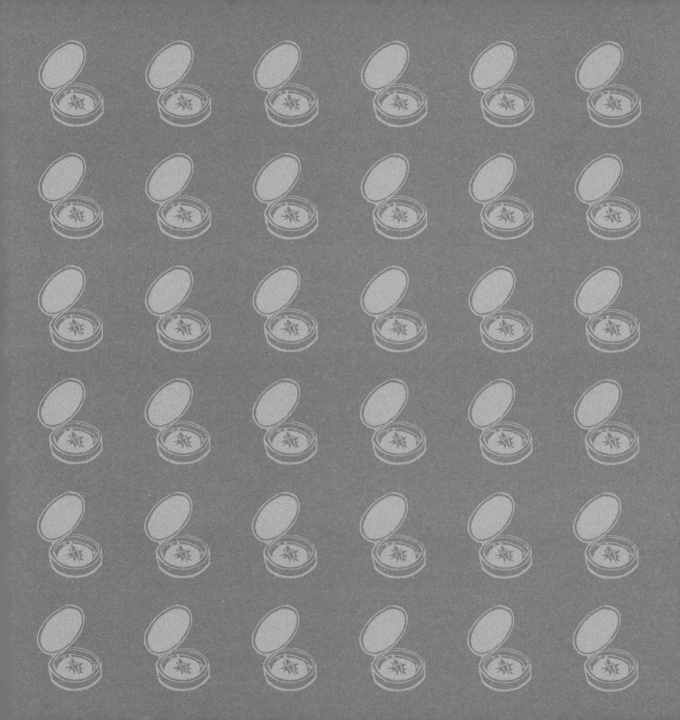

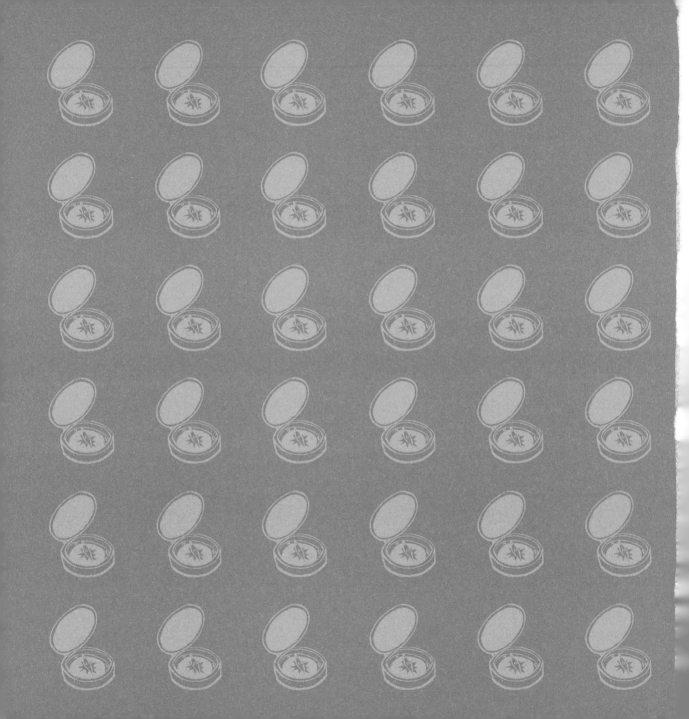

ORDINARY
PEOPLE
Change
the
WORLD

I am
Albert Einstein

BRAD MELTZER

illustrated by Christopher Eliopoulos

DIAL BOOKS FOR YOUNG READERS an imprint of Penguin Group (USA) LLC

I am **Albert Einstein.**

Ever been called weird? Or different?
That's what they thought I was.
On the day I was born, my mom was actually scared since she'd never seen a baby with such a giant head.

It didn't get easier.
I did things my own way. In my own time.
I didn't speak until I was three years old.
And when I did, my speech was so odd,
our maid used to call me . . .

Some say I took longer to speak because I didn't think in words. I thought in pictures.

Even when I did speak, I'd practice each sentence in my head, silently moving my lips and whispering to myself, until I had every word right.

When I was little, my cousins ran around
and played games outside. I liked playing alone.
I did puzzles, fed the pigeons, or just
watched my toy boat sail in a water pail.
When they saw me, other people
called me . . .

But the biggest moment in my young life came when I was four or five years old and sick in bed.
To cheer me up, my father brought me a compass.

I was fascinated by how the compass worked. No matter which way my father turned it, its needle always pointed north.

Nothing touched
the needle, but somehow
the compass "knew" where to point.
Like it was guided by an invisible
force.
Right there, I could feel it:
There was something behind
things, something deeply hidden.

The world . . . the stars . . . even outer space with all its planets . . .

The whole universe had its own order.

That compass made a deep and lasting impression on me.

It showed me that life has mystery. The universe has mystery.

And it made me curious. Why did the universe behave the way it did?

By the time I was nine years old, I would make complex structures with my blocks . . .

. . . and tall houses of cards.

It took persistence. And patience.

But I never gave up.

My sister would watch as I'd build them fourteen stories high.

IT'S GONNA FALL.

I'd even see the structure in music as I played my favorite instrument—the one that always helped me think: the violin.

Today, people say I was a genius.
But back then, teachers thought
I was a daydreamer.
One even told me . . .

When I was in sixth grade, on Thursday nights, a medical student would come to our house for dinner.

Like the compass, that geometry book changed my life.

By the time I was twelve, I was doing all different kinds of math, like geometry and algebra.

By fifteen, I was onto something called calculus.

Soon after, I mastered the entire math curriculum.

Did that mean I always did well at school?
Ask my father.
HE GOT GOOD GRADES... AND A FEW BAD ONES.
THAT'S RIGHT! EVEN EINSTEIN GOT BAD GRADES.
IN COLLEGE, HE FLUNKED A COURSE IN PHYSICS...
... THE STUDY OF MATTER AND ENERGY.
I WAS BORED.
YOU GOT THE LOWEST GRADE IN THE CLASS!
YOU **DO** KNOW I'M GOING TO INVENT THE THEORY OF RELATIVITY, RIGHT?
GO TO YOUR ROOM.

But even I didn't know I was on the verge
of my greatest breakthrough.

I was twenty-eight years old, just sitting at work as the thought occurred to me.

When a person falls—like a man falling off a roof—he doesn't feel his own weight.

Close your eyes. You can picture it too.

As the man falls, if he opens his pockets, everything inside floats there next to him.

That may sound weird . . . or different . . . but for me, it was the happiest thought of my life.

Why?

Because it sparked an idea that helped me link motion with gravity. (Gravity is the force in the universe that keeps us from floating away.)

It took me eight years of hard work—eight years of asking hard questions—to figure it out. But I did.

From there, I began to question ideas that most other scientists thought were true.

I didn't agree with what most people believed.

In the beginning, other scientists wouldn't listen.

Sometimes it's hard to get people to go along with you—especially when you discover something new. But I promise you, if you keep at it . . .

It'll be worth it.

In my life, I was always thinking.
Always asking questions.
But the most important one I asked was:
Why?

Never stop asking "Why?"
Never stop trying to figure out how the world works.
And never lose that feeling of excitement as you try
to find the answer.

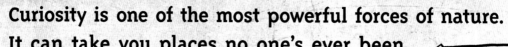

Curiosity is one of the most powerful forces of nature.
It can take you places no one's ever been,
and let you do things no one's ever done.
Will that make you weird? Or different?
Who cares if it does?
Every single one of us is different.
No one on this planet is just like you.

DREAM

I am Albert Einstein.
I will never stop being curious.
And I hope you won't either.

The more questions you ask, the more answers you'll find.
And the more beauty you'll uncover in the universe.

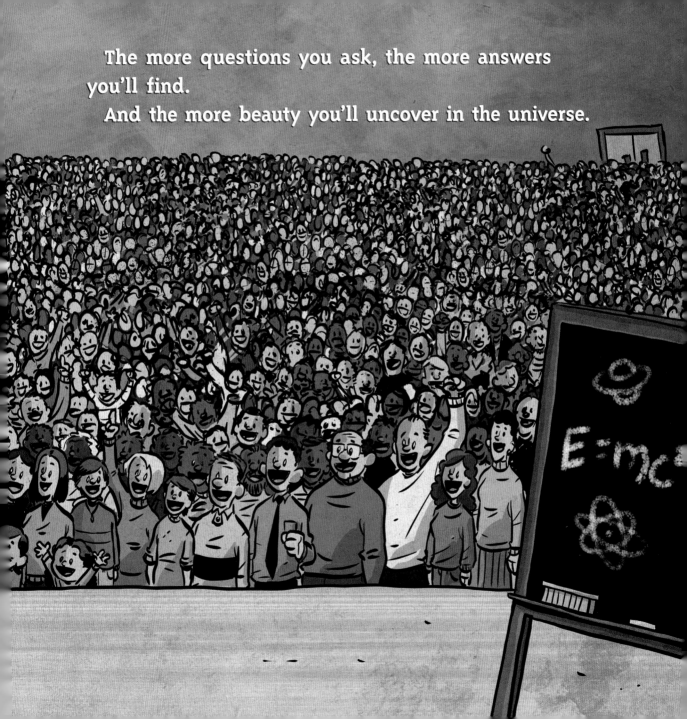

"The important thing is not to stop questioning. Curiosity has its own reason for existing. One cannot help but be in awe when he contemplates the mysteries of eternity, of life, of the marvelous structure of reality."

—ALBERT EINSTEIN

Albert as a boy with his sister, Maja

Albert the sailor

Timeline

MARCH 14, 1879	1896	1900	1905	1908
Born in Ulm, Germany	Enrolled in Zurich Polytechnic at age 17	Received teaching diploma	Received PhD from University of Zurich	Began college-level teaching

Albert
on a bicycle

This famous photo of
Albert was taken on his
72nd birthday

1919	1921	1933	1940	APRIL 18, 1955
His theory of relativity was reported and he became famous around the world	Received the Nobel Prize in Physics	Emigrated to the U.S. and renounced his German citizenship	Became a U.S. citizen	Died at age 76

For Cori,
the girl who was different than everyone else,
the girl who was smarter than everyone else,
and the girl who made my life by bringing order to my universe
—B.M

For my father, Christo,
my first hero and the person who didn't flinch when
I said I wanted to grow up to be a cartoonist
—C.E.

SOURCES

Einstein: His Life and Universe by Walter Isaacson (Simon & Schuster, 2007)
Albert Einstein: And the Frontiers of Physics by Jeremy Bernstein (Oxford University Press, 1996)
Albert Einstein: Physicist & Genius by Lillian E. Forman (ABDO Publishing, 2009)
Einstein: Visionary Scientist by John B. Severance (Clarion Books, 1999)
Einstein: The Life and Times by Ronald W. Clark (William Morrow, 2007)
Einstein: A Life in Science by Michael White and John Gribbin (Simon & Schuster, 1993)
Einstein: A Biography by Jürgen Neffe (Farrar, Straus and Giroux, 2007)

FURTHER READING FOR KIDS

On a Beam of Light: A Story of Albert Einstein by Jennifer Berne (Chronicle Books, 2013)
Odd Boy Out: Young Albert Einstein by Don Brown (HMH Books, 2008)
Who Was Albert Einstein? by Jess Brallier (Grosset & Dunlap, 2002)
Albert Einstein: The Miracle Mind by Tabatha Yeatts (Sterling, 2007)

DIAL BOOKS FOR YOUNG READERS
Published by the Penguin Group • Penguin Group (USA) LLC, 375 Hudson Street, New York, New York 10014

USA | Canada | UK | Ireland | Australia | New Zealand | India | South Africa | China
penguin.com

A PENGUIN RANDOM HOUSE COMPANY

Text copyright © 2014 by Forty-four Steps, Inc. • Illustrations copyright © 2014 by Christopher Eliopoulos

Library of Congress Cataloging-in-Publication Data
Meltzer, Brad. • I am Albert Einstein / Brad Meltzer ; illustrated by Christopher Eliopoulos.
pages cm • ISBN 978-0-8037-4084-6 (hardcover) • 1. Einstein, Albert, 1879–1955–Pictorial works–Juvenile literature. 2. Physicists–Biography–Juvenile literature. I. Eliopoulos, Christopher, illustrator. II. Title. • QC16.E5M448 2014 530.092–dc23 [B] 2013047226

Photograph on page 37 taken by Sophie Delar. Page 38: Photo of Albert and his sister courtesy of Hulton Archives/Getty Images; photo of Albert in boat courtesy of *New York Times*/Redux. Page 39: Photo of Albert on bicycle courtesy of the Leo Baeck Institute; photo of Albert on his 72nd birthday courtesy of Bettman/CORBIS.

Manufactured in China on acid-free paper • 10 9 8 7 6 5 4
Designed by Jason Henry • Text set in Triplex • The artwork for this book was created digitally.

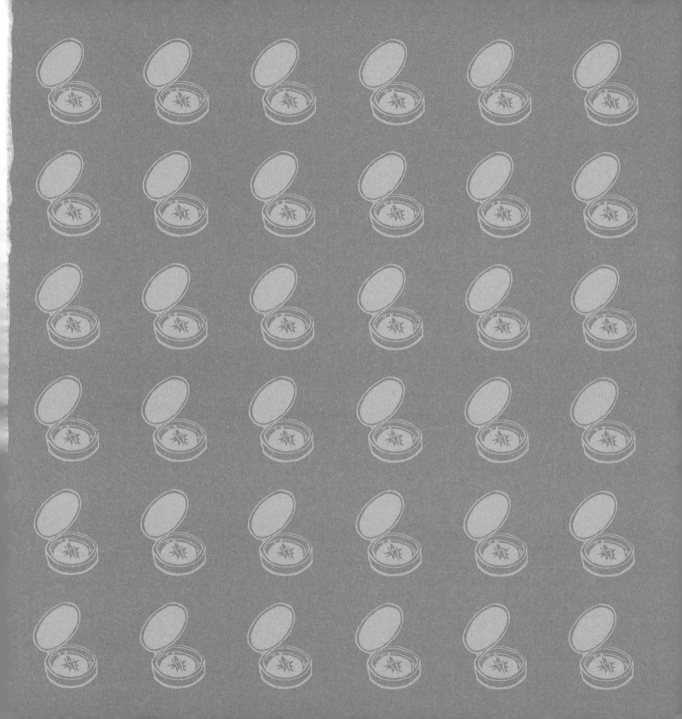

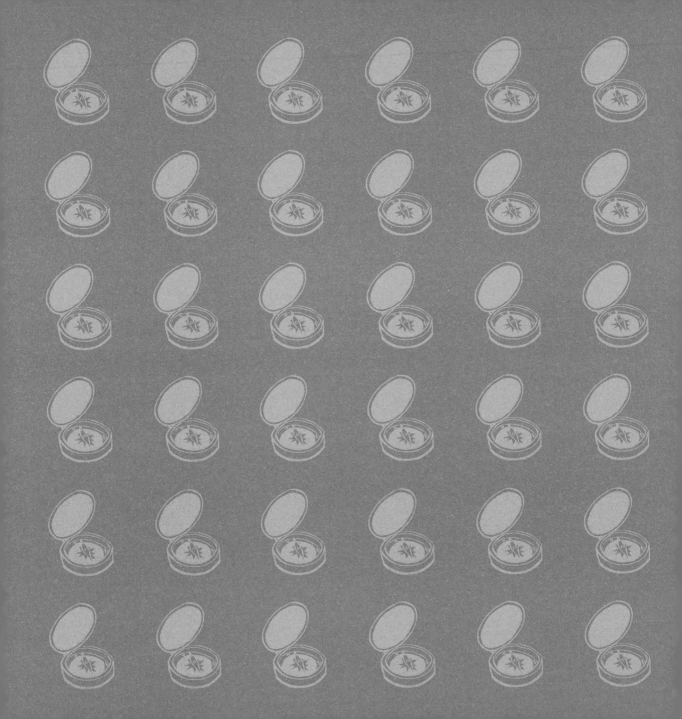

ORDINARY
PEOPLE
CHANGE
the
WORLD

I am
Amelia Earhart

BRAD MELTZER

illustrated by Christopher Eliopoulos

DIAL BOOKS FOR YOUNG READERS an imprint of Penguin Group (USA) LLC

For Lila,
my daughter,
who makes me feel
like I'm soaring

—B.M.

For Audra.
My Life,
My Co-pilot,
My Hero
—C.E.

I am **Amelia Earhart.**

When I was little, people told me that girls should wear dresses and play with dolls.

They said we shouldn't have "unladylike" adventures.

I didn't agree.

In fact, when I was seven years old, my sister and I decided to build our own roller coaster in our backyard. We placed two planks of wood up against the side of our tool shed.

The cab was a wooden packing box with roller-skate wheels attached to the bottom. We greased the wood with lard so we'd move super-fast.

Of course, I got to ride first.
This was my moment.

I still remember the wind in my face.

My stomach seemed to sink.

I was flying!

The crash was loud and
noisy and messy.
It certainly wasn't ladylike.
But it was awesome!

It wasn't the last time
I would fly.
    As I got older, I went to
many air shows.

When I was twenty-three years old (but still a kid at heart), my dad took me to meet Frank Hawks, a man who would eventually set many of his own flight records.

For ten dollars, Hawks agreed to take me on my very first flight.

For ten minutes, we flew through
the sky and out over the Pacific Ocean.
   By the time I was two or three hundred
feet off the ground, I knew one thing:
I had to fly.

To save for my flying lessons, I worked as a truck driver (which wasn't ladylike either) . . .

a stenographer (which is a fancy-schmancy word for someone who writes down what people say) . . .

and even a photographer.

Most important, like that day on the roller coaster,
I dared to do what so many said couldn't be done.

I became the first woman to fly across the Atlantic Ocean—and then the first woman to fly *by myself* across the Atlantic.

Back then, people took boats to get to Europe, sailing for weeks. Planes were still a new thing. In fact, on the day I took off, one magazine ran an article that said women would never be able to fly that far.

But I did.

To do it, I had to fly for fourteen hours and fifty-six minutes with no rest, no break. Sometimes the sun was so blinding, I could barely see where I was going.

In the process, I also broke the record for crossing the ocean in the shortest time, doing it faster than any man or woman ever.

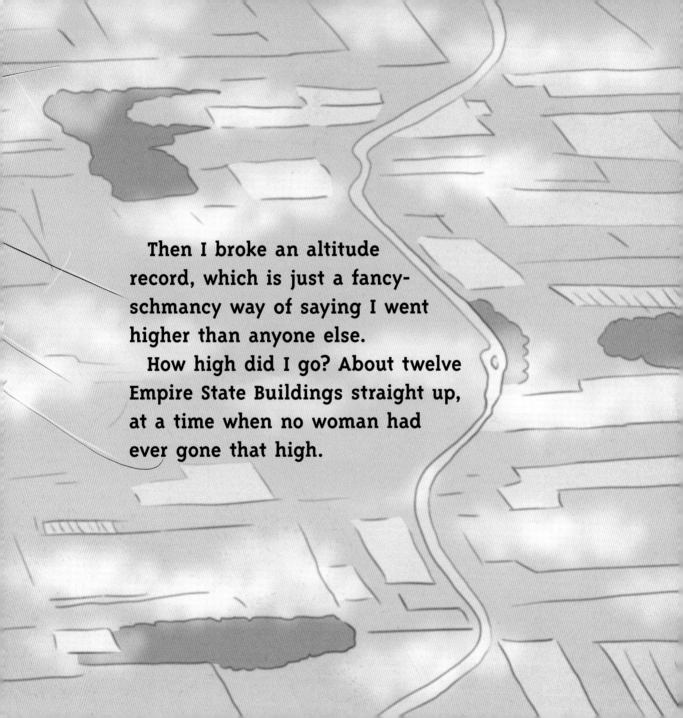

Then I broke an altitude record, which is just a fancy-schmancy way of saying I went higher than anyone else.

How high did I go? About twelve Empire State Buildings straight up, at a time when no woman had ever gone that high.

In my life, I took many flights.

Never let anyone stop you.
Whatever your dream is, chase it.
Work hard for it.
You will find it.
It is the best lesson I can give you.

I am Amelia Earhart.
I know no bounds.
And I hope you'll remember
that the greatest flight you'll
ever take, is the one no one
has tried before.

"Never interrupt someone
doing what you said couldn't
be done."
—AMELIA EARHART

Amelia, age 7

Amelia in the cockpit, 1936

Amelia with her first plane, the Kinner Airster biplane, which she named *Canary*

Timeline

JULY 24, 1897	DECEMBER 28, 1920	JANUARY 3, 1921	JULY 1921
Born in Atchison, Kansas	First airplane ride	Started taking flying lessons	Bought her first plane, *Canary*

Frank Hawks, pilot
who first took Amelia on
an airplane ride

Neta Snook,
Amelia's flight
instructor

OCTOBER 22, 1922

Broke the world altitude
record for women

MAY 20–21, 1932

First woman to fly solo
across the Atlantic

1932

Published her memoir,
The Fun of It

JUNE 1937

Began an attempted
flight around the world

JULY 2, 1937

Disappeared over the
Pacific Ocean

. . . .

SOURCES

The Sound of Wings: The Life of Amelia Earhart by Mary S. Lovell (St. Martin's, 1989)
Amelia Earhart by Doris L. Rich (Smithsonian, 1989)
"Missing Woman" by Judith Thurman, *The New Yorker*, September 14, 2009
AmeliaEarhart.com: The Official Website

FURTHER READING FOR KIDS

Amelia and Eleanor Go for a Ride by Pam Muñoz Ryan (Scholastic, 1999)
Who Was Amelia Earhart? by Kate Boehm Jerome (Grosset & Dunlap, 2002)
Amelia Earhart: More Than a Flier by Patricia Lakin (Simon & Schuster, 2003)
Night Flight: Amelia Earhart Crosses the Atlantic by Robert Burleigh (Simon & Schuster, 2011)

. . . .

DIAL BOOKS FOR YOUNG READERS
Published by the Penguin Group • Penguin Group (USA) LLC, 375 Hudson Street, New York, New York 10014

USA | Canada | UK | Ireland | Australia | New Zealand | India | South Africa | China
penguin.com

A PENGUIN RANDOM HOUSE COMPANY

Text copyright © 2014 by by Forty-four Steps, Inc. • Illustrations copyright © 2014 by Christopher Eliopoulos

Library of Congress Cataloging-in-Publication Data
Meltzer, Brad. • I am Amelia Earhart/Brad Meltzer; illustrated by Christopher Eliopoulos. • pages cm. — (Ordinary people change the world) • ISBN 978-0-8037-4082-2 (hardcover) • 1. Earhart, Amelia, 1897–1937—Juvenile literature. 2. Women air pilots—United States—Biography—Juvenile literature. 3. Air pilots—United States—Biography—Juvenile literature. I. Eliopoulos, Christopher, illustrator. II. Title.
TL540.E3M45 2014 629.13092—dc23 [B] 2013010559

Amelia on page 36 and young Amelia on page 38 photos courtesy of Getty Images • Amelia photo on page 38 (bottom) and Neta Snook photo on page 39 private collection of Karsten Smedal, courtesy of Ames Historical Society • Amelia in cockpit photo on page 38 courtesy of Purdue University • Frank Hawks photo on page 39 courtesy of San Diego Air & Space Museum

Manufactured in China on acid-free paper • 10 9 8 7 6 5 4
Designed by Jason Henry • Text set in Triplex • The artwork for this book was created digitally.